Clothing Memoirs of a Wannabe Cowgirl

Remembrances of Growing Up in the 1960s and '70s

Donna Harlan

iUniverse, Inc.
New York   Bloomington

Clothing Memoirs of a Wannabe Cowgirl
Remembrances of Growing Up in the 1960s and '70s

Copyright © 2008 by Donna Harlan

All rights reserved. No part of this book may be used or reproduced by any means, graphic, electronic, or mechanical, including photocopying, recording, taping or by any information storage retrieval system without the written permission of the publisher except in the case of brief quotations embodied in critical articles and reviews.

iUniverse books may be ordered through booksellers or by contacting:

iUniverse
1663 Liberty Drive
Bloomington, IN 47403
www.iuniverse.com
1-800-Authors (1-800-288-4677)

Because of the dynamic nature of the Internet, any Web addresses or links contained in this book may have changed since publication and may no longer be valid. The views expressed in this work are solely those of the author and do not necessarily reflect the views of the publisher, and the publisher hereby disclaims any responsibility for them.

ISBN: 978-0-595-52160-9 (pbk)
ISBN: 978-0-595-62879-7 (cloth)
ISBN: 978-0-595-62223-8 (ebk)

Printed in the United States of America

Clothing Memoirs of a Wannabe Cowgirl

How Clothing Experiences Shaped the Fabric of My Heart, Soul, and Mind

Donna Harlan

This book is dedicated to my past, present, and future family, with thanks to those who taught me well and gave me love; with joy to my husband, daughters, and son-in-law, who make me proud; and with hope for those who will come after.

Preface

We've all had to wear things we don't like, and we've all worn things that were wonderful. Sometimes the external fabrics of life can transform the internal nature of who we are and how we think. We associate great experiences with what we were wearing at the time. Conversely, we may not want to wear clothing again if we had it on during a bad day.

Because we learn best through experience, clothing can be a great teacher. We learn to express ourselves with fewer words if people know that what we look like on the outside matches what is under our skin. We learn that we can't really fool people into thinking we're someone else just because we dress differently than who we are. We learn about the character and nature of other people as they react to our appearance. We learn who our true friends are when we're not much to look at.

Growing up in the sixties and seventies as a middle child in a family of girls is an experience that I wouldn't trade for any amount of money. Because my parents cared much more about my integrity and character than my appearance, my attitude toward physical beauty found a wonderful resting place between obsession and disregard.

My goal in writing this book is that you reflect on your personal experiences and how they shaped you and your thinking. My guess is that you will come across some forgotten events that should be remembered and some days that have been tucked away in the corners of your mind. Reviewing our personal history allows us insight into our development, and that insight can be empowering as we make choices about who we want to become. Becoming is a lifelong process that requires a strong fabric in our emotional makeup. I hope this book and your own remembrances will bring a smile to your face, warmth to your heart, and a new passion for continual becoming.

The Elementary School Years

The Cowgirl Suit

I don't know how long the cowboy era lasted, but I know it was cool to be a cowboy or cowgirl in 1962, the year I was in first grade. "I want a *cowboy* outfit, not a *cowgirl* outfit!" is how I expressed my vehement rejection of skirts. The outfit simply had to have pants.

Christmas came, and with it came the *cowboy* outfit. It had pants—hallelujah! It also had a red-checked shirt similar to the one my dad wore. That made it even better. I'm sure I jumped rope a little better (I was already good) and ran a little faster with it on. It changed my life. It was a power suit.

I'm sure my parents did not purchase that outfit intact. It's my guess that it was either made by my grandmother or purchased in pieces and put together. Of course, at the time I thought it was made by Santa's elves. Knowing now that it took that extra effort to please me helps me understand how Mom and Dad valued my opinion more than teaching me to conform. They may have later thought they had created a monster, since I received a baby doll from Santa the next year, rather than the BB gun I had asked for.

The hat and boots were icing on the cake. My spirit came alive inside that outfit. It defined me—my spirit for freedom and adventure. I remember sitting and reading *Cowboy Sam* over and over until I felt I could lasso the herd single-handedly, smell the bacon frying on the open fire, and taste the pancakes served at breakfast. I laughed a little longer and louder when I wore that outfit. I'm still a cowgirl at heart, ready for the spontaneous events of the day and bringing more than enough enthusiasm to share with anyone who is without.

The Lost Birthstone Ring

Tonsillitis was a way of life for me in first grade. I was familiar enough with being sick that the most frequent words out of my mouth were, "Would you get me (fill in the blank)?" I expected to be waited on and enjoyed the attention, which was probably part of the reason that my parents decided it was time for a tonsillectomy. I didn't have any fear of the surgery, because it was all explained to me very positively with emphasis given to the unlimited amounts of ice cream I would be allowed to eat after the surgery. No one told me I wouldn't want to eat it.

The looks between my parents told me that something wasn't quite right, but I didn't know enough to ask questions and only later learned that they were familiar with a situation in which a young girl died from a similar operation because of anesthesia. The confidence that they portrayed to me was masking their personal fear.

A beautiful, light green birthstone ring was waiting for me after the surgery. It was love at first sight—my first real ring. It would have been almost painful to take it off for the night, so I slept with it on; but in the morning it was gone, having slipped off. Tears and grief followed the permanent separation, and I knew it was probably in a garbage can somewhere, swept up and unseen. At the time I was not familiar with the stages of grief, but I'm sure that I went through all of them: denial, anger, bargaining, depression, and acceptance.

That ring will always "belong" to me though. The memory of it is probably stronger than if I had never lost it. The ring still speaks to me today, reminding me of my parents' love. Some things can never really be lost.

Donna Harlan

The Red Canvas Shoes

My mom was a bargain hunter, and she was pretty good at it. The thing about bargains is that you can't wait to make up your mind, so there's a little risk involved in the purchase, even if the amount spent is small. In this case, it was probably about twenty-five cents. Mom imagined the red shoes to be cute, partly because they were cheap and partly because they were my size. She bought them, complete with their pointed toe and little elf look. They were made of red canvas, and a second, striped material formed a folded-over look on the top of the shoe. This image is burned into my brain.

"Aren't these shoes adorable?" Mom asked with a look of pure joy on her face. If my face betrayed me at the time, she knew that I thought the shoes were ridiculous. I hoped they wouldn't fit, but I quickly discovered that it is impossible to "think" your feet into being too small or too big for a shoe. The act of slipping my foot into the shoe seemed like an eternity, and I'm sure I heard dramatic music like something composed by John Williams. I knew how Cinderella's stepsisters felt, except that I wanted the shoe not to fit.

Mom was pleased. I was not. In my mind, I had no choice but to wear the shoes the next day, and while I didn't set out to destroy them initially, recess came and brought an opportunity too good to miss. Stepping into the red, clay mud, I initially drew back, being neat by nature. Then the idea presented itself so clearly that I formed my defense before I even ruined the shoes: "But we were just playing tag, and I wasn't thinking. I forgot I had them on." I managed to stain them beyond repair.

I was probably as pleased initially with my control over the situation as Mom was of her purchase the day before. She didn't say a lot—just looked at me with that "yeah, sure" look that mothers do when they automatically recognize a lie. She no doubt was thinking, *This is the same child who never comes home with a spot on her clothes.* Her disappointment was obvious. My pleasure with myself quickly faded, and I saw that my lack of honesty was painful to Mom. The end result of not wearing the shoes (and the great loss of a quarter) would have been the same either way, but being honest would have been a better choice of action than being deceitful, which can be just as ugly as elf shoes.

The Joy of Orange

Wearing orange made me feel more interesting and alive. I didn't know the word *sanguine* at the time, but orange brought out the sanguine in me. About the time I was in second grade I had an A-line linen dress with an orange center and brown sides. I think "color-block" is the term, though I didn't know that at the time. The orange was a soft shade, and I was sure, even at seven, that I had on the perfect dress in both taste and comfort.

"Are you wearing *that again* today?" was the first remark my family had for me when I chose to wear this dress. The question never caused me to second-guess or rethink. I would have glued it to my body and even taken a bath in it if I could have. I don't remember my younger sister wearing it, so it's possible that I wore it out or that she (and everyone else in the family) got so sick of looking at it that it was retired from the Childress' household. I would still wear it. It was truly elegant.

Luckily, there were other orange clothes in my life. My eighth grade year I had a wonderfully trendy two-piece dress. I honestly don't remember whether I made it or my mom made it, because we often collaborated when we sewed. The multicolored, knee-length dress had an empire waist and short, puffy sleeves. The second piece was bright orange and solid. It also had an empire waist but was sleeveless like a vest and covered about three-fourths of the length of the dress. My youth minister at the time made a passing comment about liking the dress, and I sucked up the compliment like a vacuum and stored it permanently for future reference.

The only school picture I ever really liked was taken when I had on an orange sweater. The burnt orange v-neck was timeless and classic, and it had an intriguing history as far as I was concerned, having been worn by my mom when she was a child. My sisters and I "found" it in our attic and resurrected it from its cedar chest grave.

It's hard not to smile when you see orange. Orange demands a positive response, so it's a good standby to have in the closet for those days when you feel a little melancholy and need a brighter outlook. If you get lucky, someone will throw you a compliment that you can chew on for the rest of the day—maybe the rest of your life!

Donna Harlan

The Green Corduroy Pants

The green, wide-wale corduroy pants were poorly constructed, even to the eye of a nine-year-old girl. They might have been bought *for* me, but they weren't bought with my body in mind. I was scrawny; the pants were wide. I was tall; the pants were short. Unfortunately, the elastic around the middle made them "fit." I imagined Aunt Sarah saying, "Oh, look, Joe, these pants have elastic. They're perfect!" I am confident that my aunt and uncle wouldn't remember this purchase, which they made for me more than forty years ago. It was seemingly insignificant—just a small gesture of love. Thank you so much! I will take the memory of the pants to my grave.

My parents responded with equal love and gracious acceptance, assuring them that I would enjoy wearing the pants, beginning tomorrow. I suppose this act of receiving and speaking on my behalf was intended to reward my dad's brother and his wife for their travels from Florida to Tennessee to see us. I admit these relatives are wonderful, sweet, thoughtful people, and I'm sure that buying gifts for three girls is difficult when you have only one child who's a boy.

I tried the pants on for all to see, and I'm convinced that everyone in the room knew the choice was a poor one; but instead of stating the obvious, smiles were exchanged around the room, and it was agreed that I would wear the pants to school. I wanted to scream, "Hasn't anyone read 'The Emperor's New Clothes'? Doesn't anyone have the guts to be truthful here? The Emperor is naked, and these pants look ridiculous!" I restrained myself.

I have no clue what they brought my two sisters or my parents, but the green pants were a severe lesson in obedience and humility that I will never forget. I wore them to school the next day. I don't remember if anyone else said anything about the pants. I probably wouldn't have heard them if they did, because I was too busy listening to the voices in my own head. "I can't believe it's only 9:00. This is the longest day of my life." "I can't wait to get home, show my aunt and uncle the pants, and take them off." "I wonder if people think we're poor." "I wonder if people think that I think these crazy pants actually look good on me."

No doubt my parents knew the experience wouldn't kill me, and it didn't. It was character-building, to say the least. What did I learn? I learned that looking ugly isn't the end of the world. I learned that my friends aren't nearly as concerned about my clothing as I am. I learned that life is sweeter when I don't argue or embarrass others and that sometimes it's better not to state the obvious.

School Pictures

All the things we wish we could forget about our looks come rushing back to memory when we look at elementary school pictures. I've often wondered where my mom was on the mornings I prepared for picture day. Furthermore, where was my teacher, and didn't she care? What was the photographer thinking? Didn't he have a comb handy? Long before zigzag parts were popular, I had the original zigzag part in my fourth grade picture.

Of course, now I can see the "beauty" of these pictures. They captured the true personality and essence that often remains elusive in professional shots. I'm actually glad to get a glimpse at remembering how unconcerned I was about my physical appearance before the age of twelve.

It's a rare individual who grows up without being awkward along the way. The fact that a camera somehow captured vividly that pervading awkwardness makes me wonder how I appeared in motion and in real life. Being unsure of myself often caused me to appear socially challenged, and I remember a relative telling me that I was rude once because I ignored something that was said. I responded with an attitude, "Yes, I am rude, crude, impolite, and socially unacceptable." The shock on her face was priceless, and I think that my parents even found my response somewhat amusing, although they didn't admit it. Fortunately, my faux pas occurred before the time when video cameras captured all the significant (and less than significant) events in children's lives.

I'm still not photogenic, but I have learned a few social niceties along the way, and I keep a comb handy.

It Doesn't Pay to Copy

Joanne came to Indian Springs Elementary when I was in the fifth grade. She was always a mystery to me and someone I admired in a different way. She made popularity seem attainable to almost anyone. Sharon, the most popular girl in the class, became friends with Joanne the day she arrived. Joanne wasn't attractive at all, and she really didn't have any charm or warmth. What she did have was maturity, social grace, and a put-together look. She also chose the "right" friends. I'm sure her parents had money.

Joanne had a multicolored, striped jumper that I coveted. I was sure this jumper was one of the magic keys to her look, which also included soft-teasing in her short bob hairdo. I had never known a fifth-grader who teased her hair. I told my mother about the wonderful jumper and how I needed to have one like it. This wasn't a small request, considering that we didn't buy a lot of new clothes, and my mom worked everyday until five o'clock in addition to doing all the cooking and cleaning.

It would have been easy for her to say no, especially since I rarely helped around the house. I'm not sure if I was persuasive or my mom was just easy, but we went on a search. Maybe she felt she owed it to me so that I wouldn't grow up with a complex about being the middle daughter. I remember getting in and out of the car many times at different shops, and finally as we were both about to wear out we found something similar. Actually, it wasn't all that close, but it fit the verbal description I had given my mother, and of course she had never seen the coveted jumper.

At this point, Mom was determined to take something home and make me wear it whether I liked it or not. I was in a corner. I had to at least pretend to like it. I didn't hate it, but I knew it wasn't the jumper of my transformation. I suppose that ultimately I wanted to try on Joanne's skin. I wanted to know what it felt like to have her confidence and grace.

I wore the jumper several times. It was okay, like most of my things, but it didn't define me the way the red-checked shirt did in the first grade or the orange and brown dress did in the second grade. Copying someone may be the most sincere form of flattery, but it isn't the road to personal identity.

I've never, ever dripped of social grace, but warmth comes easily to me. I have a different set of gifts than Joanne—gifts I've learned to appreciate. I've never teased my hair, but I do have a simple, short bob that is easy and not contrived. I've never worried about choosing the "right" friends other than to reject users. I have no idea what happened to Joanne, but I imagine her throwing dinner parties for the "right" people and then giving tours of her Southern Living home. I'm quite sure she still teases her hair and speaks with grace and confidence. I'm still the same in most ways, too, except that I've learned that it doesn't pay to copy or covet.

Don't Wear Sundresses in Early Spring

Being an optimist has its drawbacks. If I wake up and the day is warm and sunny, I assume it will *stay* warm and sunny. On the other hand, if I wake up and the day is cloudy and cool, I assume it will *become* warm and sunny. This thinking has gotten me into some bad situations on different occasions.

In March of my fifth grade year I awoke to find that spring had arrived overnight. There was a warm, gentle breeze, and the sun seemed friendly and playful. I knew exactly what I wanted to wear that day. I had been waiting for the first opportunity. The dress was made of thin, soft cotton. It was white with a small, repeating pattern of a purple flower. It slipped over the head and tied at the shoulders with purple ribbons. I knew it would be a perfect day.

"You need to take a sweater with you to school." I ignored Mom's comment as I ran out the door, pretending I didn't hear it. Why weigh myself down with things I didn't need?

Recess was not optional, and the class went outside every day unless it was raining or snowing. Sometime between eight o'clock and one o'clock, the temperature must have dropped about thirty degrees. The gentle wind had turned harsh, and the sun had quit playing. It was a long recess, and I was too cold to run or play, which of course would have helped a little. All I could do was stand still, shaking and turning blue.

"Didn't you bring a sweater with you?" was all the sympathy my teacher had for me. I thought, "Wouldn't you like to go inside for the rest of recess?" would have been more appropriate.

I would like to say this one incident cured me of poor clothing choices based on the weather, but the scene has been repeated often enough, even as an adult, that I am finally a believer in weather forecasts. I keep a jacket in the car just in case I need it, and I confine my optimism to areas other than the weather.

Donna Harlan

Packing for Summer Camp

Starting around the age of ten and continuing every summer until I was fifteen, my sisters and I went to church camp for five days. Leaving on Sunday afternoon and returning home on Saturday morning, I knew the daily routine by heart, and for the most part I loved it.

Everything started the week before. Campers needed fresh clothes for outside activities each day, a swim suit, and six dresses for worship—one for each evening. Basically, this was my entire wardrobe, so it really wasn't that difficult to pack. The biggest challenge was finding the dress for Friday night. According to camp tradition, the dress should be white for the special candlelight service. White symbolized purity, so there was some spiritual significance to having the right dress.

I always loved having an excuse to get something new, and this was a necessity, of sorts. I looked forward to putting on my white dress, as did all the campers. It made us feel beautiful on the inside and the outside. It didn't matter that we were all girls. We were dressing up for God and for worship (and for each other too). It created a sense of expectation, a greater sense of the presence of God, and a unity among all the girls.

I doubt that we could ever recapture that time, but I am grateful for it. I'm grateful for the crisp, morning air and exercises in the parking lot, followed by singing "God Bless America," saying the pledge, and eating runny scrambled eggs with weak Kool-Aid. I'm grateful for long, missionary talks; for crafts that revealed my lack of talent (and interest); for cold mountain streams that fed our swimming pool; for banging screen doors and afternoon thunder boomers. I'm grateful for rustic cabins that were filled with peepholes, laughter, music, and late-night talks. I'm grateful for barbecue corn chips and root beer and goofy camp songs.

Most of all, I'm grateful for the chance to grow up with a sense of innocence and simplicity.

Pantyhose and Book Satchels

I got my first pair of pantyhose in the sixth grade, and I wanted to make them last as long as they could. "I *promise* I won't ever run them if you let me wear them to school!" I said to my mother. The only thing crazier than making such an unpredictable promise is thinking a twelve-year-old knows what she is talking about. I'm sure Mom knew they wouldn't last long.

They actually did make it through several days, which was amazing considering the construction of old school desks, pencils, cafeterias, recess, and boys. I probably became somewhat prideful about how long this pair was going to last, so when my leg came into contact with a younger child's metal buckle on his book satchel (this was long before backpacks), I wasn't very happy. This was the death of my first pair of pantyhose.

I later learned why older women wear the kind you can't really see through that make loud, scratchy noises when they walk. The hose are not only almost run-proof; they also hold in all the bulges that sixth graders don't have. Of course, there are still some unanswered questions here: Should sixth graders wear pantyhose? Should anyone ever have to wear pantyhose?

Sewing: The World of Possibilities

I was ten or eleven when my mother taught me how to sew, and I don't mean sew on a button. With her coaching and occasional deliverance from seemingly unfixable problems, I made an entire dress myself, which I wore and actually liked. Obviously, there was some pride wrapped into the dress. "Guess who made this dress!" was probably the first thing out of my mouth when I wore it. It was a simple pattern, like most dresses were then—a round neck, sleeveless, straight with a zipper up the back. It was white with a blue stripe every half-inch or so, and the only challenge was a half-inch trim that cut across the bodice of the dress.

The dress was made from a garment we found in the attic. Going to the attic to find fabric was almost sacred. I could feel my heart start to race with excitement because I knew the world of possibilities that was there, and everything was free. Moving from the stage of spectator to my mom's creativity into the realm of sewing myself was almost like a rite of passage. Luckily, most of the old dresses I found in the attic had gathered waists with yards of material and huge hems that were included for growth spurts. With a pair of scissors and an iron, we created new bolts of cloth. Making the first cut was the beginning of a great journey, made even richer with the knowledge that this fabric already had a history. It contained untold stories of the people who wore the original garment.

Stopping at the fabric store was the only thing that rivaled this great adventure in sewing. First, Mom and I would choose a pattern after long and careful deliberation. "Is this too hard for me?" "How long would this one take to make?" "Do you like this?" "What kind of material would you use for this?" What incredible patience and vision Mom had, knowing that it would have been easier in the short run to have made the clothes herself. No doubt her goals for me were more long-term than what I was going to wear during the upcoming season.

Patterns were inexpensive then. After we located the pattern in the correct size in the metal drawers arranged by manufacturer, we walked slowly and carefully through each aisle—looking, touching the fabrics, visioning, reading the notions list on the back of the pattern. After careful thought and another endless barrage of questions from me, we made our purchase, and I knew it would all come together, just like the picture on the front.

I stopped sewing after I got married and discovered the joy of credit cards and instant gratification. Sometimes I think back and start to wonder. I find myself at the fabric store flipping through books in search of a pattern. Then I roam around the store imagining all the possible creations, realizing the number is somewhere close to infinity. Of course, I could take one of those possibilities home and make it happen, but I don't. It's enough just to dream.

I miss my mom. She died with ovarian cancer when I was only twenty. We were bonded, like Velcro, and creating things together made that bond even stronger.

Even though I don't sew often, her example of creating and dreaming is with me every day.

The Junior High Years

Never Say Never

Prior to my twelfth birthday I swore I would never spend any time doing the things that women do to make themselves look good. I would not style my hair or wear makeup because that would be a huge waste of my important time.

I'm not sure what I needed time for, since I didn't help around the house much, had very little homework, and few extracurricular activities. I played outside quite a bit and tried to persuade my neighbor Rick, who was about four years older than I was, to play football with me. He wasn't interested. I mean he *really* wasn't interested. "Don't you need to go help your mom with something?" was just one of many questions he asked that didn't require interpretation, but I wasn't easily dissuaded. Riding bikes with my sisters and best friend, Cathy, took hours at a time, and my perfect day would have been having a rotten apple fight with anyone who would participate, either willingly or unwillingly.

I don't know when the first roller went into my hair, but once I started, there was no turning back. I endured many nights with hard plastic curlers, which made me understand more about Jacob in the Bible, knowing that he slept with a rock for a pillow. It was a great relief to know what my hair was going to do the next day rather than having to use a wet comb to fight the unintended effects of bed head.

I discovered that there was actually an element of fun in making myself look better—egg white on my face for a mask, mayonnaise in my hair for conditioner. Teen magazines were full of interesting ideas and suggestions to assist in the pursuit of beauty. Having two sisters made it three times as fun.

Before the age of twelve, chasing boys was literally that. I chased Harvey all over the playground in the first grade, and his fear of being caught and subsequently kissed made him the fastest kid in the class. After the age of twelve, chasing boys meant sleeping in curlers and wearing mascara. It was fun in a different kind of way. The girls did the chasing, but the boys did the catching, or at least they thought they did.

Donna Harlan

A Defining Moment

It was difficult for me to admit that I'm a "one look" kind of girl, but I came to terms with it in the seventh grade. Before the late 1960s our school system allowed girls to wear pants through the sixth grade, but upon entering seventh grade girls could wear only dresses or skirts to school.

I would never have challenged this, but evidently someone else did, and I was quick to agree. The administration decided to let students vote on this option, and by a slim majority, the student body agreed that girls should be allowed to wear pants to school.

I knew immediately what I was going to wear the next day, and assumed others did, too, but only Rene and myself showed up in jeans the next day. I wasn't discouraged and enjoyed the comments. "I can't believe you wore jeans to school. You're so brave. I was scared to, because I didn't think anyone else would." What an easy way to become a hero!

Jeans became my second skin, and I didn't even have to become a rebel for that to happen. They are still my favorite thing to wear, and I've worn out several dozen pairs. Some people claim that jeans aren't comfortable, but I know they just haven't found the right ones yet. "Uncomfortable jeans" is an oxymoron to me. Fortunately, I've had other "Renes" in my life who shared my passion for jeans. Rita always said she wanted to be buried in her jeans and a yellow (her favorite color) t-shirt. Julie's love of jeans is legendary, just like mine.

Even if I know I'm going to be at home all day, I put on jeans and fix my hair and makeup. This is my one look—the definition of my appearance. It has been through style changes—hip-huggers with holes, peace symbols and wide leather belts; high-waist, trouser-type jeans with cuffs and a crease; basic Levi's; capris; jeans that look like leggings; stone-washed, boot-cut Gap jeans; and summer-weight denim for hotter months.

I almost changed my college major to social work when I found out that jeans could be worn to work and that flashiness and jewelry were discouraged. It would have been a good match for my one look, as well as for my heart. Perhaps our looks originate from further within than we realize.

Asking for Opinions

I didn't usually ask for opinions about how I looked, mainly because my goal in dressing was to be comfortable. Alice, my younger sister, was always much more creative in her dress and was frequently asking Karen, my older sister, and me what we thought about how she looked. After the question "Which of these two outfits should I wear?" was answered, Alice's response was usually something like "Well, I'll wear the other one then, because you must not want me to look good!" or, "You're just jealous of me!" Sometimes her response was, "You don't like me!" Naturally, we found this hilarious, and our laughter (in her face) only made the situation worse.

Asking another female for her opinion about clothing doesn't solve any problems. If you give the "correct" answer, the other person doesn't believe you and thinks you are just trying to make her feel good, which might be the case. If you give the "wrong" answer, you risk hurting the relationship, since the purpose of the question is really just for agreement.

Unfortunately, people sometimes offer opinions that aren't solicited. Sharon told me in the seventh grade that I didn't wear mascara, as if I wasn't aware of it. Obviously, this was meant as criticism, or at the least, correction. It is doubtful that the motivation behind it was to make me look better. "Freelance" opinions are rarely offered in good will, especially by twelve- or thirteen-year-old girls. Girls this age are among the cruelest of all living creatures, which is a fact known by most people. World wars could be fought by girls this age using emotional weaponry, and the fallout could be just as dramatic as that wrought by grown men using guns.

Girls of all ages have opinions about how everybody looks. We can't help it. It's just in our nature. I've spent more than enough time in airports, amusement parks, and malls giving people "grades" for their looks, sometimes even verbally with a friend. "What do you think—a four or a five?" I've given a few eights and nines, but I don't remember ever giving a ten, except to Vanna White when I spotted her in California one year. Never mind that I was probably a five or six at the time of the "game." Although it sounds like a cruel activity, it's really just a fun way to pass time. I've never passed judgment on parenting skills, character, work ethic, or spirituality based on anyone's looks. I'm not offering unsolicited help. I'm just keeping my assessment skills sharp.

Donna Harlan

Being Invisible

Anyone who is bashful at heart like me knows the desire to become invisible at key moments; for example, ages twelve through fourteen in their entirety. I felt like there were times I was able to do this, being the stereotypical middle child. The position worked for me. It would be easy to ask, "Which came first, the position in the family or the personality disposition?" I could argue either way, since I've fully outgrown my fear of attention.

Growing up, I could always manage to divert attention to Alice, with her beautiful blonde, curly hair and artistic abilities, or to Karen, who was incredibly mature and responsible. It was easy enough to sense when I was "invisible" and when I wasn't. The problem was that if I became aware of being visible at a moment that was highly uncomfortable, my face would reveal my emotional state, usually by turning red. I have the opposite of a poker face. Practicing lying hasn't improved my ability to do it, so I've pretty much given it up.

Other things that worked in my favor were my dishwater blonde hair and my completely average physical size. Thank you, God! I was awed by Susan, who developed early and was a head taller than anyone else in the seventh grade. Susan wore a loud pink, polka dot dress that I couldn't have pulled off even with my normal development. Her confidence was amazing. Karen fell into this category as well, which only made being second in the family that much harder to pull off gracefully.

I was never completely sure if people could read me as well as I imagined, but in my mind I knew that if I was attracted to a boy there was a flashing neon sign on my forehead that said, "I like you!" It was scary. Sensing this, I would turn red, which made the problem cyclical. My fear of being in such a situation made it almost impossible to be friends with boys that I liked. Not having any brothers, I related to boys as if they were aliens. I'm guessing there were a few boys along the way who thought I had been sunburned for life.

Stinky Gym Clothes

My junior high gym clothes were stinky for two reasons. First of all, I hated them. They were ugly and unflattering, and who wants to change clothes at school when you've spent so much time getting dressed to begin with? The shorts had cuffs that hid the elastic underneath—elastic that prevented exposure of unmentionables during exercises. If you were unfortunate enough to have gym in the morning, your dilemma was even greater, because too much physical activity or sweating might ruin your look for the entire day.

The second reason my gym clothes were stinky is that I didn't take them home to wash them very often. Washing our clothes was actually part of our gym grade, but luckily, my gym teacher liked me even though she was fully aware of my bad habits. Another part of our grade was taking a shower, which was also an area of challenge for me. I found it exciting to see how much I could get away with. I would carry my clothes into the shower, pull the curtain, turn on the water, and step back out of the way, allowing just enough mist on my body to look like I might have showered, and then I would put on my school clothes before leaving the shower stall. "Did she or didn't she?" was my goal, but I don't think I fooled a lot of people. I did "get away" with it grade-wise, which made it more fun than following the rules; but in retrospect, following the rules would probably have been at least as easy, and I would have had the added benefit of being clean the rest of the day.

Donna Harlan

Giving and Receiving

Mrs. Page was one of the most well-known people in the church I attended as a child. She was known for one reason—her faithfulness. I don't know exactly what her affliction was, but she had a special place on the first row on the left side of the sanctuary. Underneath that pew was a small leather footstool that stayed there all the time waiting for her to show up. She would have someone pull it out for her each week. Most of the time I saw her she was sitting, but that didn't stop her from visiting with and encouraging others.

My parents always spoke highly of her, and I knew they had a good relationship with her. One year at Easter she gave my sisters and me gift certificates for new dresses at a local department store, long before gift certificates were in vogue or even common. I'm not sure what motivated the generosity, but it was a gesture of thoughtfulness I will always remember. Maybe she knew that my mom often stayed up sewing into the early hours of the morning. Maybe this event happened after my mom was diagnosed with cancer. It's impossible for me to reconstruct the time frame in my mind. Maybe my parents had financial problems that I wasn't aware of. I often heard my parents' quiet voices for long periods of time after I had gone to bed, and I would lay there wondering what they were talking about. In the morning there was never any clue that anything was wrong, so I would never have known if money problems were an issue; it's unlikely that anyone else would have either.

Choosing the dresses was like a party. Mine was made of yellow linen with a broad, white collar and white cuffs on the short sleeves. Wearing them was even better than choosing them, but I imagine that the greatest joy for anyone in this scenario was the joy that Mrs. Page felt when she saw us wear the dresses. I've been on both ends, and while receiving is truly wonderful, there are times when the joy of giving can't be exceeded.

The Power of Compliments

Buddy Wood, one of my teachers in the youth department at our church, took every opportunity to compliment and encourage me, which made him one of the most significant adults in my life as a teenager. He's no longer with us on the earth, but he left me with many positive memories. It was no secret to me that he liked me as a person and that he saw my potential. "You look good in red. That's your color. Doesn't she look good in red?" That particular compliment wasn't really about what I had on. It was about him teaching me to wear confidence. His compliments weren't limited to how I looked. I heard, "Great serve!" during volleyball, and I remember, "That's the best chocolate cake I ever had." He was generous, perhaps even lavish, with his compliments, but their frequency didn't diminish their value. I needed them like I needed air. At times I felt I would have choked without the right words to keep me breathing.

Mr. Wood taught me more through encouragement than I could have ever learned in any lecture or Bible study class. His words were certainly more powerful than any correction, advice, or guidance would have been, though I wasn't without the need for those things. He probably didn't realize what a powerful impact he had on my life. His unspoken but powerful "Fear not!" was conveyed to me as a friend and mentor rather than in the form of a Sunday school lesson that was disconnected from my life. In this way he was the voice of God to me. I pray that my life is an echo of Mr. Wood's words: "Fear not!"

Donna Harlan

Queen for a Day

Each year at the church in which I grew up, there was a ceremony at the end of the school year during which girls who had participated in "Girls in Action," a weekly mid-week program, would be recognized and honored for their achievements. There were levels of advancement, much like in Girl Scouts, and each level meant receiving a corresponding token.

When a girl had completed the necessary steps for "queen," she received a crown. The ceremony involved being presented to the church body and quoting scripture or making some other presentation. The appropriate dress for a queen was a long, white dress. Mom made me a simple, long, white dress out of a brocade fabric, complete with a yellow velvet trim around the short sleeves, neck, and bodice. The dress is hanging in my closet today, one of the few articles of clothing from my past that is too meaningful to get rid of.

More memorable than the event, the dress, the crown, or the recognition was the work that went into reaching the goal. During that year I learned to love visiting nursing homes, which has paid off well for me since my dad is in one today. I learned to enjoy making cookies or cakes for shut-ins, and learned the value of putting the "right" things inside my head. Much of the memory work that I did during that time has stayed with me and shaped my life and decisions. I have experienced the power of memorized scripture on many occasions in my life at just the right moments. During some of my most trying times I "heard" Psalm 23 being spoken to me verbatim. Each word conveyed new and fresh meaning and seemed to fill me with energy for the tasks I was facing. Courage was restored when I didn't have any left. Remembered scriptures have kept me from doing or saying things I would have regretted later, and other verses have released me from guilt, worry, or the judgment of others. The journey to becoming "queen" proved to be more exciting than the coronation, and the distinction proved to be more internal than external. But I certainly did enjoy wearing the dress.

The High School Years and Beyond

The Problem with Having a Favorite Article of Clothing

The problem with having a favorite article of clothing is that you "can't" wear it all the time. In high school I had only about five days' worth of clothes that I liked, so I tried to wear something different each day of the week and in a different order each week. I didn't keep track of it on paper, just mentally, because I figured that if I couldn't remember something about myself, no one else would either—unless it was someone with some kind of clothes fetish. I have a friend who keeps a clothes diary just so she doesn't "embarrass" herself by wearing the same things in front of the same people all the time. She's done this for about 15 years now, and I will admit that she always looks good; but she's not a jeans kind of girl, so I can't use her for personal comparison.

In high school I had a brown linen pantsuit and a navy polyester pantsuit that I was sure I looked wonderful in, although now I wonder how anyone ever looks good in a pantsuit. (Keep in mind that even men wore pastel-colored leisure suits made of polyester at the time.) I wanted to wear these two things all the time, but I had to stagger my unfavorite clothes into the mix so that I looked normal in my dressing habits.

I once read a story in a devotional magazine that troubled me somewhat throughout the years. I found it difficult to process my feelings about the moral. A woman felt convicted by God about spending money on clothes and about calling attention to her looks, so she picked out her favorite clothing item—a blue dress—and got rid of everything else in her closet. She bought several more of the same dress and wore them all the time so that no one ever noticed her clothes, and she never had to think about what to wear.

This sounds lofty, but I would get tired of seeing her in the same thing all the time, and I would also feel guilty because I didn't wear the same thing all the time. I'm sure she was following her heart, and I completely applaud her desire to please God. I'm sure my heart is greedier than hers, not that I'm proud of that, but sometimes I want to wear pink; sometimes I wear purple; occasionally I wear red. Every color of the spectrum is found in my closet just in case I need it for the mood I'm in. I hope God understands. I'm assuming His creativity and diversity gives us some idea of His love for beauty. Wonder if He has a favorite color?

Donna Harlan

Miniskirts

Skirt lengths in the early 1970s varied from short to very short. In 1973 I had a student teacher in chemistry who was definitely in step with the times. The fifty-minute class was interspersed with frequent pencil droppings by the boys, and these "accidents" usually occurred as the college student was walking by the "clumsy" students' desks. I don't remember that she ever commented about their butterfingers, but she had to know something was going on.

Alice, the creative one in the family, had the problem of skirt lengths all figured out. She simply let Mom decide how long her skirts should be, which she quickly and compliantly said "yes" to; but before she even got on the bus to go to school, the rolling at the waist began. Three rolls were about maximum unless she wanted to look deformed at the waist. Of course, rolling also required that Alice remember to unroll as she got off the bus.

My parents were probably somewhat wise to her habits, but like the student teacher, they chose to remain silent. And I wasn't going to rat about any of the secrets that worked for me as well.

My Dislike of Uniforms

Nurses used to wear only white instead of the colorful scrubs they wear today. In addition to their starched, stiff dresses, they wore caps, thick, white hose, and chunky, white leather shoes. They looked very official and serious. As a child in the 1960s, I would look at pictures of nurses and wonder why anyone would choose to wear those white hats. How could nurses keep them on and move fast enough to help people who were hurting? Besides, they looked like something you would make in an advanced origami craft class. I assumed that the people who wore them enjoyed being recognized for their skills and position, but I would just as soon have my hair dyed purple.

The white dresses were okay, but only because they usually had deep pockets that held interesting medical things. My mom wore a dress like that to work every day. She worked for a pediatricians' office, so her pockets were always filled with suckers and notepads from pharmaceutical companies. My sisters and I were the glad recipients of these treasures at the end of her working day, so it made waiting on her after school a little more tolerable. The last fifteen minutes before she got home always left me feeling anxious about her safety. I never really understood that grown-ups didn't have a bell for dismissal at the end of the day. When she finally walked through the door in the evening and asked, "Which flavor do you want?" in reference to the Dum Dum suckers in her pockets, I would heave a huge sigh of comfort and relief.

I found the white hose and shoes atrocious. Why would anyone construct a pair of clunky, white leather shoes? It's like wearing flashing sirens on your feet. What about the women with big feet? Maybe it's more difficult to trip or fall with them on since they can never lose sight of where their feet are.

I maintained my dislike for uniforms and was able to buck the system the summer of my junior year in high school. I worked at a camp in North Carolina and was supposed to wear a uniform that I found incredibly ugly. It was a pastel color that defied description, perhaps "soft peach" or "nude." The knit fabric hung loosely on my body, screaming for darts or a belt or anything to make it interesting.

My friend Linda and I had matching outfits that we used in a puppet group, and the camp director kindly allowed us to wear those outfits for the salvation of our pride. It didn't make washing tables any easier, though, and sweeping under beds was a concept with which I was completely unfamiliar. "Don't you know how to sweep under beds?!" was screamed at me more than once by the demonstrative Italian who was our immediate supervisor. I apparently didn't master these tasks since my good friend Joe nicknamed me "Useless" that summer.

I wore a fast-food uniform for one day. In 1980, before the technology explosion, employees were required to yell orders to those cooking, and the only thing worse than wearing the uniform was screaming, "Fries!" I returned the uniform the next day.

I hate to admit it, but I still feel sorry for people in uniforms, even though I'm pretty sure they don't feel sorry for themselves. Most of them probably love knowing what they're going to wear each day. There are a lot of uniform wearers out there, so please don't take offense. You would probably hate wearing jeans every day. My kids actually tell me that I have a uniform of sorts—jeans and polo shirts. That works for me.

Outfits

Outfits are not in the same category as uniforms. Outfits are cool. I'm quite sure my motivation for joining a few organizations while growing up was simply to wear the outfits. I also joined a few clubs in high school just to get my picture in the yearbook more often. As soon as pictures were made, I lost interest. I was even an officer in the drama club, but the play was way too much work, so that didn't stick. Granted, this all sounds very immature, but no one was pushing or prodding me to stick things out, so I just followed the whims of my teenage heart.

Sing-Out Kingsport was a large singing group that was easy to join and easy to drop out of—the kind of gig I was always looking for. I wouldn't want to label myself as a quitter, but the grass always seemed a little greener from the other side of the fence. I didn't mean to be fickle, but how would I know if I wanted to do something unless I tried it first? That was my philosophy growing up—one that I have tried to battle at least to the point of realizing that it takes a while to figure out whether I like something or not. My friend George has a favorite saying that has helped me navigate this constant dilemma in my life: "You can't be good at something unless you're willing to be bad at it first!" Thanks, George, I needed that!

Sing-Out participants wore red knit pantsuits. I thought they were amazing, so as soon as I joined I made it a point to get the fabric and make the outfit. The gig didn't last long, though. Once I was at rehearsals, I looked like everyone else and there was no special attention or status unless I was performing. I knew I didn't have any hope of singing a solo, so the attention level would be low. Some amazingly attractive guy whose name I don't remember sang "John David Sebastian Smith" with such emotion and perfection that no one else was going to get much billing anyway. No one wore their outfits to school, so belonging to the group was not like being a cheerleader or being on the dance team, which automatically included attention as part of the deal.

I had some outfits that I wore when I was doing puppets for church youth performances, and because they were just ordinary clothes I was able to wear those to school, which made having the outfits more exciting. I tried being a candy striper, but labeling test tubes for hours at a time didn't make the outfit worthwhile, and of course no one would ever wear that to school.

My junior year I participated in an evangelistic crusade that originated at the high school. I got a great blue dress out of the deal, but there actually was much more to this gig. My heart was in it. I'm a Jesus freak. I even forgot what I wore during the crusade.

The Surprise Party

Birthdays in my family were celebrated in meaningful but not extravagant ways—a favorite meal at home, a relatively inexpensive gift, cake and ice cream, and the "Happy Birthday" song. I can count on one hand the number of birthday parties involving non-family members I've had in half a century, which is fine with me.

So when I woke up on the morning of my sixteenth birthday, I was in no way suspicious of what my family had in store for me that day. Since I didn't have much planned, except some shopping, I decided to do things the easy way. I just sprinkled a little baby powder in my somewhat dirty hair and brushed it out. Then I threw on something casual and uninteresting. I have always had a tendency to do things the easy way. I love to be so comfortable that I actually forget what I have on. Accessories such as jewelry, watches, and scarves seem to weigh me down and beg to be left in the drawer. More often than not I give in to their pleadings, as well as the pleadings of my hair ties to be used for the purpose of a ponytail.

If I have to change the way I walk, move, or think throughout the day because of my clothing or accessories, then my day is less than perfect. My goal in dressing is to be so comfortable that when someone compliments the way I look, I have to look down to see what I have on. This has happened on several occasions. It is worth noting that *comfortable* and *ugly* do not mean the same thing. I would never be able to forget about being ugly, nor would I be ugly on purpose. If it weren't for the pictures that were taken on this birthday, I wouldn't have a clue about what I had on.

On this summer morning Alice kept telling me to take my time—wash my hair and put on something nicer. Naturally, I just took offense. That's what sisters do with each other, especially if it's "your" day.

Shopping was uneventful, a day I would have quickly forgotten had it not been for what followed. I walked into the house and heard, "Surprise!" My girlfriends were there with big grins and gifts, and I was completely amazed that this had happened without any clues (although they had been there; I just hadn't noticed). Of course, no one really cared about how I looked, and I've enjoyed the remembrance of the day more thoroughly because of the dirty hair story, although I have tried to guard against repeat performances. I'm now more prepared for surprises, but I hope to make them memorable for reasons other than my appearance.

Thank God for Laser Eye Surgery

My pride and subsequent rejection of glasses probably caused my reputation to suffer in high school. I wouldn't wear them when I was walking down the hall, which meant I couldn't recognize anyone until I was fairly close to them. I wouldn't have been the first to speak since I was unsure of anyone's identity until he was five feet away from me. I probably didn't always realize when people spoke to me first either. High school students are quick to label other students as "stuck-up," so the risk factor for not speaking to friends is high and carries consequences. It probably helped that my friends knew I couldn't see, and the constant squinting was a reminder to them that I wasn't avoiding their gaze—just trying to find it.

It didn't occur to me that being friendly would probably have gotten me a lot more "points" than not wearing glasses. Contacts worked for a while, but if I was having a bad contacts day during a formal occasion I usually opted for red, teary eyes with a dress rather than glasses. I could never decide whether I got more "points" for contacts with red eyes or for glasses and clear eyes. I guess I always felt like I could "explain" the red eyes. "Do you ever have allergy problems? Mine are killing me!" is perfectly acceptable as small talk, and being vulnerable and open (within limits) seems to make people comfortable around you. Explaining your need to wear glasses is like explaining why you're ugly. "Sorry I had to wear these glasses because I can't see" just doesn't work well as a conversation starter. It's not generally done, and if it is, it usually takes away points, instead of adding them.

The easiest and best way to score points socially is to listen, ask questions, and care about what other people say. It's quite likely that the person you're talking with isn't even aware of whether you have glasses on or not. Listening to the person you are talking with works for both parties, because both people enjoy the conversation and leave feeling good about themselves. The worst strategy for "points" is talking about your accomplishments and how much you know, otherwise known as bragging.

At any rate, laser eye surgery has taken away my fear of being "pointless" at formal social events, and for that I'm quite thankful.

Donna Harlan

Wanting Other People to Look Good

"What would you think about keeping three girls from the children's home over the Easter break?" Mom asked us one year after she had heard about the opportunity. "The girls don't have anywhere to go, and the staff needs a break. They try to find homes for the weekend so everyone can have a good experience at Easter."

We kept the girls on more than one occasion. Darlene was especially memorable because of her incessant love of tomatoes, which we grew in our backyard in the summer. Tomatoes were present on our table at every meal, including breakfast, and we taught Darlene the joy of eating a tomato biscuit, which is a hot, buttered biscuit with a sweet, ripe slice of tomato in the middle. She found them delectable and talked about tomatoes all the time. The other girls were enjoyable but more reserved, and they didn't leave the same lasting impression that Darlene left.

The photograph that was taken that first Easter weekend of my sisters and me with the girls also left a lasting impression. The three of us had on new dresses, but the other girls didn't. The staff from the children's home explained to us prior to the weekend that buying them new clothes was optional, and I know my parents felt like they couldn't afford to do it. They probably didn't want to spend more on them than us for fear that we might resent them or be jealous. I would have preferred for them to have new clothes rather than myself, and the picture made everything even more apparent to me. Standing beside someone, both literally and figuratively, makes her needs and your own blessings more obvious.

Clothing Memoirs of a Wannabe Cowgirl

Why You Should Keep a Few Pieces of Clothing from Your Past

Everyone should keep a few key pieces of clothing from their youth or young adult days so that their children can understand a little more about them. Likewise, everyone should probably get rid of a few articles of clothing so their children won't understand everything. Seeing some of my mom's old things in our attic was a revelation to me about who she was before I knew her. My idea of who she was became less static, and I began to view her as her own person apart from the relationship she had with her family.

Mom eloped when she got married (I think she was around nineteen at the time), and she wore a short, blue satin dress that was probably a size two or four. I'm sure she was beautiful, without a wrinkle on her face, and I'm sure her hair was full and long and silky. She was always beautiful to me, but knowing how beautiful she must have been at this age made me realize how proud I was of her.

Mom also wore capri pants and halter tops a long time before we ever knew what they were. She was a fun person, and apparently she wore fun clothes before she started wearing a white nurse's outfit to work every day. I have a picture of her standing in the snow with a bathing suit on. I found the picture so intriguing that I took one of myself in a bathing suit in the snow and encouraged my girls to do the same. I would love the tradition to continue for many generations. Maybe someday my great-, great-, great-granddaughter will publish a book with all these pictures. I would be smiling from the other side, knowing that mom's lighthearted spirit was being honored. I'm not sure whether Mom passed this love of life on to me by example or whether it's in my genes, but I hope to pass on the joy of living to those who follow.

Donna Harlan

Wash Your Hair at Least Once a Week

If I could have ordered my hair, it would be long, dark, and silky, and maybe a little coarse so it would be easier to style. It's hard to love your natural hair color when your first remembrance of its description is "dirty blonde." Combine this with the fact that as children we often washed our hair only once a week. It made me wonder what shade of blonde I would be if I washed my hair every day. I wasn't sure what "clean blonde" looked like, but I thought I would like it better than my natural color.

I've worked hard to compensate for my non-descript hair color. Risky haircuts were a way of life in high school. "It's just hair. It will grow" was my mantra. The interpretation of this was, "I know it looks bad, but you don't have to tell me. *Please* don't tell me. It's bad enough as it is."

Thank goodness for the invention of hair gel at just the right time in my life. If a person sleeps on rollers with hair gel, her hair becomes like a form of hard plastic. Unless she stands in pouring rain, her hair remains the same. I had some great plastic-like styles in the eighth and ninth grades, and the school newspaper even claimed I had the "best hair" once. For a dirty blonde, this seemed remarkable.

My most life-changing hair experience took place while living in Singapore as an adult (I didn't learn some important lessons well as a child). I decided to take full advantage of the sunny, hot days at the pool at our apartment while my husband was working and my kids were in school. I began swimming every day, and eventually my hair turned green. I decided the best way to deal with it would be to make the color a darker blonde that would hide the green, since I wanted to continue swimming.

"Could you just make my hair a little darker? More like the color of my roots?" I asked in the salon. I should have noticed that everyone there had black hair. It might have been the only color of dye they had. In fact, black is the color I got, but I didn't know what was happening until my window of time ran out and I needed to be home when my children got there, so I left the shop with black hair. My children didn't have the greatest reaction. "I like it better blonde. Do *you* like it?" The color was supposed to eventually wash out, and I thought it would be a fun experience in the meantime. I was wrong.

A few days later my husband came home from his business trip to find me with black hair. I had a big smile on my face because I truly thought the experience was funny. I thought he would appreciate the humor. I was wrong. He wanted to sleep on the couch rather than with this strange woman he didn't know.

So, I made my way back the second time and declared that some of the color needed to be stripped out. Once again, I didn't know how the process was going until it was too late. One look in the mirror at the girl with dark red hair, and I knew that I would be coming back to the shop again soon. I was beginning to understand that how my hair looks is probably more important to other people than it is to me, oddly enough. This is not what people tell you. They are lying. People have opinions about your hair. They think their opinions matter to you, whether they really do or not.

After my third trip to the salon my hair was a strawberry blonde. *Kind of cute*, I thought, and it would eventually fade a little. Swimming looked less and less appealing to me after that. I got some arm weights and began dancing in my kitchen to the music on the radio.

Donna Harlan

My Wedding Dress

Surprisingly, my wedding dress was less expensive than plenty of other clothes that I've owned since then. Because I was never really into the girly stuff growing up it didn't seem natural to suddenly spend hours picking out a wedding dress. It would have been completely foreign to me to spend the entire day doing hair and makeup the way that most brides do today.

I don't remember exactly who went with me to help me choose my dress, but I do remember Alice going. The first dress I looked at was on sale, and it was my size, so I tried it on. It fit and looked good, so I bought it. I didn't know any better. I didn't know I was supposed to spend the whole day trying on dresses, even if I ended up buying the first one I tried on.

I didn't know I was supposed to get someone else to do my hair or makeup. I'm sure I looked exactly like I did with jeans on, only with a long, white dress instead. I *did* know that it was supposed to be the happiest day of my life, and it was.

Since then, I have learned not only to shop for hours but also to thoroughly enjoy shopping for hours. I've learned all the nuances of shopping. I've learned to enjoy buying things and taking them back the next day. I can shop for a reason or no reason. I can shop quickly or at a relaxed pace. I can shop alone or with others. I can shop for myself or for someone else. I can shop when I'm happy or when I'm sad. I can shop to buy or just to look. I can help *you* shop. I can shop.

It's a good thing I got married when I did. Finding a dress might have taken years.

Being a Cheerleader

Missed opportunities are almost as important as those we experience. Long-term learning takes place when we forget an answer to a test question, and making mistakes in life helps form us into individuals that are more deliberate and thoughtful about future outcomes.

I never got to wear a cheerleader's outfit. One of the reasons I wasn't a cheerleader in high school is that I got so nervous I forgot to yell during try-outs. Crazy, isn't it? Multitasking doesn't always come easy for me, and I was so focused on my own fear, as well as the mechanics and precision of the movements, that I failed to notice that the words of the cheer were coming from my partner's mouth and not my own. I was pleased with my motions, my jump, and my smile. It wasn't until a friend asked me why I didn't cheer that I even realized what had happened. I had all the potential, but I forgot the purpose of cheering. I focused on everything but the actual reason for having cheerleaders. My focus was on myself, not on cheering for someone else.

Although I've never been a cheerleader on a playing field, I hope I have always been a cheerleader in life. Taking the focus away from me is not easy. It's a daily struggle, and I have to remind myself constantly of my purpose. One of my mentors, Fred Witty, once said to me that God could do anything through me if I could get myself out of the way. I've thought about that for more than thirty years now, and it has motivated me to get over myself. Of course, that doesn't mean that I should be unprepared. What it does mean is that my cheers are not to make myself look good or gain a position in life, but to encourage, stand beside someone else, give confidence, and say, "Fear not!" to those who need to hear it.

I hope these threads of my life have brought some meaning to your life. I pray that the fabric of your heart is always strong and weatherproof and that there is always a cheerleader in your life.

Printed in the United States
127485LV00004B/115/P